M000036523

To my beautiful muse, who has kept me on the straight and narrow, even when I wanted to go off the path. To the fans who have waited patiently for this to happen. To my parents who have loved me and made this even possible. I love and thank you all!

To truly appreciate the light, you must go through the darkness. Pain hurts us all. But shared pain, is pain healed, and to heal is to be happy, and to be happy is to love. Know that you are not alone because love connects us all...

Spring

Unruly

These losses of words are still heard from the voices of the page.

I've been screaming for help for so long, and the silence has turned to rage.

I need help, I'm trapped inside my mental. The outside is a facade. Haven't been to the doctor in years but I could still pass a physical.

I've been giving advice since high school, but in the same breath it became my vice.

How I tell you not to do something, but I turn around and do it.

I care more about you than I care about myself.

Friend once told me I'm a bank and I got to have a balance. But I give so much and I'm short on wealth.

Surrounded by love, the thing people would kill for. But still I hunger for more.

My whole life I wanted to be different and now the only thing I want is to be the same.

Like how you allowed to lash out, bow out, call out, fallout, and tell bout without a consequence. But, I sit here and stay so understandable.

Makes me sick that everyone can be themselves even if they make mistakes. But I can't, because I'm afraid to taste it. Afraid of what the world will think, when in actuality they cared less.

But I too want to act careless only without caring less. I'm just a tall mess that never got sorted out.

Guess this is just the cost of all complacency that I have happily paid. Good Lord look at the unruly mess I've made.

Sweet Suicide

Your favorite lie was I love you.

You never knew anything about me.

Did you know my favorite color was blue?

For most of my childhood I wondered what type of man I will grow up to be.

Now, I spend most of my adulthood living care free.

Can't blame it all on you, I've got my part to play too.

Kept my faults to myself because I didn't want to disappoint you.

Wish I could have told you somethings.

Somedays I woke up not even wanting to be alive.

It's ok communication is a 2-way street and we never knew how to drive.

So how can you teach me when you don't even know yourself?

Kind of makes sense now that I only came around when I needed some of your wealth.

Saw me physically and everything was fine, but did you notice my mental health?

I was a diseased minded person that had been traumatized by unkind words.

To go back in time to stop us from meeting might have saved me some tears.

Because honestly you never liked my writing or my ideas.

So, scared of you that I couldn't tell you my fears.

So, jaded on the word family that blood doesn't mean nothing.

When I say that everybody gets weird from my aunts to my cousins.

You got a big part to play in that like your name was Jordan

The only trait I got from you is the Hoarding.

I hold onto all these things when I should just let go.
I'm going to change that and go right for the throat.

The kid with daddy issues is no more.

Here lies a boy who fought with all his life.

On that faithful day, the boy died.

A man rose from the sweet suicide.

Best Foot

My best foot forward always seemed to move me back. Always wanted to be different but my bad habits kept me on track.

When I close my eyes, I can see your disappointment. All those times you saw me, and you never charged me for appointments.

The promises I made to you, I just flushed them down the toilet.

Pain filled me up because I appreciated everything you've ever done. Your heart was always open, and I just choose to run.

I remember when you were the only one I could talk to. I opened up and gave my life to you, only to discover it's a pain to my own soul.

All you ever did was give and all I did was to take. Oh!!! how I wish I could go and buy a clean slate.

Told you I love you, but my actions showed that it was all lies. Wanted to be better but honestly, I never tried.

You never gave up on me, even when I gave up on myself.

You ripped things from me that I depended on, just to tell me they were things I never should have depended on.

You showed me what I must give to the world can't be wasted, still victories to come that I have yet tasted.

I want to thank you for teaching me lessons that I can appreciate now. I want to apologize as once a disobedient child.

Looking back, I overcame things that I've done. Your heart was always open, I just choose to run.

You

I think I took a tumble; I think I fell

It was you that got me wrapped in your spell.

I never met anybody like you before.

Is this feeling real or is it fake like jersey shore?

It's like when I'm with you nothing else matters.

You make all the stress, and the irritation to all go away.

Are you a superhero come to save the day?

Your voice is so heavenly every time you speak.

I swear the angels rejoice every time you do.

The way you got me feeling. It's so strong.

But it's too soon, I can't say it just yet.

How do I tell you without saying... "IT"

Maybe I'll write you a poem and call it...

Dreamers

They used to make fun and bully me in school.
I had no friends and I was so uncool.

The girl I liked didn't even notice me dude.
She paid more attention to the dumb boys who were rude.

I'd stay up late wondering why I couldn't be liked.
Every day was a struggle, felt like I'm losing the fight.

And my parents? My parents just don't understand.
They can't see the vision of my master plan.

A ball in my hand was all that they saw,
can't be anything else if you're black and tall.

And every day a new goal and occupation
a room of FMs, I'm a AM station.

And my broken voice always went unheard.
Silence and to follow orders were always preferred.

Critics everywhere, I had to escape these fiends
stuff, my thoughts in my book bag and escape to mine.

There's always a hater trying to put down your dreams.
And the world throws enemies unseen.

20/20 vision but you can't see all your obstacles.
20/20 vision but you can always see your vision.

Can't let nobody ever take your drive.
No one should ever take what you got inside.

They say dreamers don't have a sense of reality.
But at least we have individuality.

These are the whispers of the words of wisdom
Not too many people ever hear them.

The ones with sense you never see them.
The ones without say that's not a problem.

Barely can read about any good deeds.
Drama and negativity clutter your news feed.

Not saying dreamers are picture perfect.
But I promise the image we paint sure is worth it.

Wings

These streets they'll never tell me what I'm worth.

Been against all the odds since my birth.

The words are gospel, think you're sitting in church

Clipped wing, damn right I still flew even when it hurt.

Making something of yourself is a crime.

If you've been shot down, you know I aint lying.

Still I go, tackle life with the heart of a lion.

Wanting to be alone that never made me weak.

It just fueled the success that I choose to seek.

I stood for something, others stayed in their seat.

My father never cared for the dream I saw.

that's why it's been so long since the last call.

See my dreams are well within my reach.

Won't stop till I'm napping on my private beach.

And when it's all said and done, I'll lift my head and say this one's for you.

April 16ᵗʰ (2014)

Her eyes met me under the stars. She brought forth her heavenly voice, it sounded like a melody.

Her essence invaded my own, and in turn lifted me higher in infatuation with her.

If I didn't know the word perfect and I saw her I would describe her.

Mere feet away from me but it might as well be a whole continent away. Afraid of what to say.

Even though the fear was bubbling inside of me, her energy gave me strength.

I looked up at her and her eyes met mine. Felt like time froze.

I could stay here for eternity, trapped inside her gaze.

My mind started to think. What did I look like to her? Did she feel this same energy or was it all just my imagination? Because if it is, I just want to stay in this daydream a little bit longer, embracing the procrastination.

Her face turned into a smile, which in turn made mine too. I hope I don't scare her off chasing like a fool.

She looked down and up again checking to see if it was just a coincidence. But if this is what Love at first sight feels like, there is no coincidence.

I fixed my lips to introduce my love-struck self. But she spoke before I did and greeted me first.

Said her name was Jessica. And she began to explain that she just felt something warm and comforting about me since I got on the bus.

If her voice was a waterfall, then I was dying of thirst. Drinking everything that she said.

I sat there in awe when she was done. Something about her made me believe that she could be the one.

Concrete Massacre

Blood on the hands of parents who are holding a lifeless child.

Animals have more sense in the wild.

Guys stand on the corner claiming what they think is theirs.

It's a wonder that they don't start charging fairs.

Love is a meaningless word thrown around.

Everyone claims they're lost when they really don't want to be found.

Forever embraced by the bosom of ignorance.

They call it home because the home is where the lies are.

There hasn't been any heart in it since it was built.

Females embrace every other name besides queen.

and males start unwanted families anywhere a plot of land is seen.

I don't mean that a female is a plot of land

or just a tool used by man.

But they just get it anywhere they can.

Children grow up with these same values

Thinking that education isn't something to be valued.

It's not a good thing to raise your hand and be smart.

Sitting in ignorance waiting for a push like they're groceries in a shopping cart.

This is the only life they know, the only life they're showed

Little jimmy is being bullied at school.

But we're more worried about celebs life like it's cool.

The streets and Social media are a better fight promoter than don King.

All that leaves are mothers in tears and grandmothers to sing.

Black on white crime happens and my people scream racism
No matter if the black was wrong, we'll cover it like a white lie.

I have to ask aren't you tired of playing the victim?

Life is hard but what would you compare it to?

Our hands were dealt to us, it's something we could not choose.

Blood on the leaves, blood on our hands.

Nobody likes change to that's why we're still standing here in this quicksand.

Now with that being said, I hope the hungry minds are fed.

Words of the wise are rarely heard or said.

Summer

Heart Coming Soon

It felt like my hearts have been gone for the longest.

It's like it's been in the shop, preparing to come back the
strongest.

I never really was the same after it was broken a few years ago.

When it broke, a part of me went with it.

And I know it's not fair that I'm not giving you all of me.

You don't know how grateful I am to you.

You don't know what it's like to walk around years without
breathing.

But when we kiss, you breathe life into me.

I swear to you my hearts coming soon.

I'm going to love you for all it's worth.

When it finally gets here, you are going to see it beat through my shirt.

All I ask is please don't break it like the last

Hug it forever so that it'll last.

Most people don't get a second heart

And most don't get a second chance at true love

So, let's make the most of it.

And love with our all..

The Miss in You

When you're here, it's like forever summer. But when you're gone, it's like there are nothing but chills.

Your face brings happiness, your smile makes the best of the worst day.

Your love is overwhelming, it's where I love to lay.

Now, you're away and it's like I'm lacking air. It's hard to breathe.

Sometimes, I can smell your scent and it hurts because you're not there to accompany it.

It's amazing how you can love somebody so much that their very presence can have an impact on your happiness.

Soft kisses I reminisce, hugs bring nostalgia, late night talks I adore.

I miss you!!!

Tying Shoes

Being in love with you has been a journey. It's like tying shoes.

It takes some work at the beginning, somedays you just don't want to tie anything at all and just slide on some shoes.

Other times, you don't want to tie shoes at all. But you're walking over gravel and you're not scared to fall.

Then you get into it, learning how to tie your shoes and it becomes an everyday process.

1st step, you take to strings that might not always have the right length and hold them together

2nd step, sometimes one of us may fall but the other catches them.

3rd step, one of us goes through the loop which in turn makes the string even. 4th step is we cross together, the yin to my yang.

5th and final step, tightens and strengthens the bond.

Because since we got the shoe tied, we can travel together in this world called life together.

The Dedication

My heart is warm. Her love is a comforter.

My long arms wrap around to hold and comfort her.

She makes me smile, even when I don't think there's anything worth smiling about.

The times I made her blush is more than I can count.

My love for her no other can obtain.

It wouldn't change for all the money and the fame.

Her head on my chest, she said the beating of my heart is no better sound.

She gave me her heart, so I kept the love locked down.

Seeing you happy has got to be the best sensation.

So dear love, this is to you. My letter of dedication□

With Love

I haven't heard your voice yet, but I bet it's the sweetest thing.
Mama, Dada, even the alphabet you'll sing.

Play in the pool in the summer. We'll get your uncle to teach
you how to swim.
Make snowmen in the winter and zip up your coat to protect
you from the Chicago wind.

Will you be smart like your mom, or sarcastic like your dad?
Will you come to us, or solve it yourself when you're sad?
I just want to give you everything that I never had.

I'm going on about this and I haven't even seen your face yet.
Your mom's facial features and my height is a safe bet.

But when I do finally see you, I'm sure you'll show me what
love at first sight means.

I can't wait to finally meet you and hold you in my arms. I
mean I can, but I can't wait.
For you to grab my finger with those tiny little hands.

Looking into the eyes that are full of wonder.
I'll protect you from the rolling thunder, there's no need to cry.
And I'll love you forever, even when you look up at me in the
sky.

No question about where you'll be in my heart, always forever
1.
Sincerely, Dad

Destiny

Been through it all, we still hold strong.

People still say we won't last long.

Everything in the world tried to tear us apart, even ourselves.

Might not be soulmates, but we are a living destiny.

Girl before her broke my heart and I lost all emotions.

Without her knowing it, she found them, then it was up to me
to apply them.

Sorry it took so long, but I had to re-learn showing them.

Still got these battle scars, but the war is over.

Morning kisses makes my heart smile when you roll over.

Never judged you because you were as weird as me.

I gave her all of me because I've kept to myself for too long.

She asks why I still love her when at times she feels unlovable.

But I do it so you know that I love you Full time, part time isn't acceptable.

Loving you and seeing you smile gives me an otherwise un attainable wealth.

You take care of me, I take care of you and we keep the relationship in good health.

We have our days where we can't wait till the sunrise of the next day.

Some nights time just stops when we're in the moment.

Wrote her random messages of appreciation because she's God's gift to me.

I took her hand as we flew over the ocean, heading in to the horizon.

She's my best friend, my lover, my everything.

We love for better or worse and we don't even wear rings.

Sometimes she doesn't have to speak because I can hear her heart say it all.

Never hide it, our love is a mural on the wall.

Say it without love

It races fast.

It beats like a drum.

Never runs on empty, it'll last forever.

It brings so much happiness that you couldn't even   fathom.

I see it in your eyes, you never want to let me go.

You see it in my actions that's how you know.

Let our lips meet in the holy matrimony

And don't let it die till an unfortunate ceremony.

Till the sun goes or the curtains come crashing down.

Like the memory of your first time, it will always be around.

They aren't enough words to explain.

Or divine actions, just too plain.

To say just how much.

Just how much....

Purpose

Ever since I first saw you, I knew you were the one.

Been playing games my whole life, but you taught me how to have fun.

Ups and downs, arguments, going round after round.

It's been a hard, long journey but it's the happiness in you that I found.

Sometimes, I'm left speechless looking into your eyes.

At times, I get lost in them, but I'm never truly lost.

Can't wait till we walk down the aisle and confess our love in front of a cross.

Tell me how'd you got so perfect? I hope when you look at me you think the same?

Your smile, I wish I could just frame it and take it with me wherever I go, but I'll settle for keeping your heart close to mine.

What are you going to teach me next? You're my hero academia.
I'm in love with your quirk.

9 years and it feels like eternity. I'm older but you're still more mature than me.

I can't wait to see where our sun rises next. Whatever it is, I know it will be worth it to spend it with you.

August 5th (2016)

He showers me with love, and it's all appreciated.

We started from nothing, we stand in what we created.

He's the apple of my eye, yet my core is still rotten.

Wrote me half a dozen poems, half of them I've forgotten.

He doesn't deserve this, he doesn't deserve me.

I love holding his lock and key, but deep down I want to be
free.

How'd I let it get this far carrying all this baggage?

Says he loves me, but honestly, it's the idea.

How could you love someone, and want to marry them this young?

I hate how he makes me feel. Mr. and Mrs. Parker, it rolls off the tongue.

Can't crush his heart, but maybe I can have my cake and eat it too.

If I play it cool, I can do what I want to, if only I can keep him out of the loop.

I wouldn't be in this predicament if I didn't say I love you...

Letter to Mom

You always flew in to save the day and never wore a cap.

Examples of love, you're where I got it from.

Definition of courage, you're where I studied from.

Hope to make you proud one day with God's gift.

I'll put you in a house that's the size of your heart, I hope it fits.

Thankful for everything that you do, and everything that you are.

In your eyes, I'll always be your perfect little boy.

Hope I can become a better man?

I love you and appreciate you with my all.

-Sincerely, your baby boy.

Letter to Dad

Not good with saying words directly, I guess that's why most of my words to you have always been in poetry.

I painted you as the villain for the longest.

Waisted so much time, we could have been the closest.

Didn't graduate on time, I couldn't tell you face to face.

Sorry I was a kid who didn't know how to handle pressure.

Fast forward a few years and I showed you my high ACT score, you said "oh" and handed it back to me, you don't know how much I hated you for that.

But I couldn't tell you, so I wrote and wrote. Through the pain, and sobs from my throat.

You found out about sweet suicide, and it hurts to see your youngest talk about you that way.

I was hurting and putting all my anger in the wrong things but my venting only fueled the fire.

Took the death of uncle William to bring us back together. I regret that it took that to bring us back together.

Long car ride turned into our confessions. Finally, got to the bottom of some things that needed addressing.

I'm sorry for not being there and being the worst son. Sorry for not being everything you'd hoped me to be by now. Hope one day to truly make you proud.

Closest you'll ever get.

People always try to tell me what to do in life, maybe it's because I'm where they could never be in life.

Struggling to be something by coming from nothing. I don't know where my path leads but I'm planting seeds.

I just want to be remembered for doing something great and impactful. I told my dad that and he said it was laughable.

Parents just don't understand sometimes but you can't pick your family. Trying to express feelings while still sounding manly.

Sometimes, I feel like I'm the last one left, everyone's been converted but everybody has their right to be asserted.

I wish I could open up and be normal and admit the pain. But I think if I start now people would think I'm insane.

I deal with it all without a crutch, no shots or passes. It's just a war going on behind these glasses.

Life has handed me lemons and I'm posed to make lemonade, but I don't even have a pitcher or spoon to stir.

A lot of the pain is self-inflicted, mental scars on my wrist. Body is strong but mind isn't, it's on suicide shit.

But I rise above it every time. Keep telling myself that the worst is yet to come.

To look at life like chess and people as stepping stones. It's all perspective but am I wrong?

Maybe it's just the overthinking as usual, but believe it or not, it saved my life on more than one occasion.

If I gave you my mind for one day, you wouldn't even be able to keep your head up.

Heavy is the head that wears the crown. How does he keep it all together?

I ask myself the same, but loose it all at the call of the word lame. It's all such a shame.

God has plans and all I'm doing is why this and why that. And I've been answered with nothing but facts.

And this is the closest you'll ever get to a vent till I'm heaven sent.

Tears

I know my tears more than I know what's going on around me.

My cries are loud, but no one is around to hear it.

No one wants to console this lone and miserable spirit.

My tears keep me warm in the cold of night.

Scared to tell anyone of my sorrows because they might not have equal eye-sight.

I try my best to be strong and act as if nothing fazes me.

I deserve an Oscar and haven't even made a movie yet.

The world is a stage, and everyone has a role to play.

But if that's true, then who is it that comes to save my day?

Who can I bear my burdens on that I've carried for so long?

Who is willing to listen?

Who is able to afford to spend some time just to pay attention to my story?

For the moment, nobody is there. I'll just keep the weight in my heart.

Act as if I said nothing at all. These are my tears.

Outside the Lines

Use to tease me for being a nerd...

Use to tease me for being a nerd.

Called me gay because I wanted to watch wrestling instead of watching the NBA

Wanted to watch the new DBZ instead of the video of the day on BET

I didn't fit the cookie cutter of the cool kid.

Tall, shy and awkward, most of my classmates didn't have any respect for me.

They messed my head up, made me think something was wrong with me.

Didn't help when the teachers chimed in.

Came home crying one day thinking that I was a walking sin.

And all of this was in elementary, so it's only fitting that my first life lesson was elementary my dear Watson.

Once you step outside the lines of what's expected, they treat you like you don't belong.

It's sad but it's true, maybe there's a reason that ever since I was a kid my favorite color has been blue.

The day I stopped giving a damn and started embracing myself, it felt like I had been reborn.

Like a phoenix, I rose up from the ashes, tall skinny kid with glasses.

Playing video games, reading books, watching anime, doing cosplay. I'd have life no other way.

Love me for me or hate me for living my life free.

I know what it feels like to live your life under a magnifying glass, not going back to that now.

I thought I told you that the ones that had it the hardest growing up are usually the ones that end up holding the crown.

God made me, and he doesn't make mistakes, so who are you to tell me I'm living my life wrong?

But you who live your life like twitter is the bible and follow the latest fad is living right.

I look in my mirror and see myself, you looked, and you see 20 people.

I know this reality check stings, the injection is lethal.

But I look at the bigger picture and I make a masterpiece out of odd shapes and signs.

I will forever color outside the lines.

R.O.I.

I seem to be a ray of light in a lot of people's lives.

But sometimes, I have dark days and they scare me like if I was 5.

I've hit rock bottom a couple of times.

Days where nobody's words could cheer me up no matter how kind.

Depression was like an ex who couldn't leave me alone.

Misery was the girl I never wanted but still had.

I was stuck in a love triangle that I wanted no part of.

But I had to get out of my funk with some self-love.

See, I never was the type to find a blade to keep away the pain.

But I remember a couple of times when I was close to ending it all, to think back on that now is insane.

I wanted all of it to end because I couldn't take it anymore.

But the thought of all the loved ones who cared stopped me from doing it.

Knife to my throat, tears in my eyes, I couldn't make this shit up, I tell you no lies.

I thought it to be selfish to take my own life.

To rip myself away from the people who love me the most.

I walked through the pain. To the paper, I vented and with music I overdosed.

You look at me now and might see a new man.

But I see someone who faced his problems, but never ran.

I'm not proud that I let myself to even let it get that far.

But proud to stand before you as the guy who didn't let his darkness overshadow his light.

On that day, I didn't take my own life.

So I write this poetry to let you all know because I've been holding on for too long.

I share my pain, fears and triumphs.

I'm not perfect but I'm not afraid to show my imperfections.

I'll Be Late

The road is clear, I walk alone and have no fear.

Opportunity is knocking. Girl of my dreams is for the taking. No cockblocking.

The trail has been blazed but I like to detour.

It's all in front of me but I refuse to run and grab it.

Destiny awaits but I'll be late.

I only make things harder for myself. Not afraid of success.

I'm always complicated. Never simple.

I'll be late getting there. But I'll arrive on time.

Only the true thinkers will make sense of the last line.

Always called a late bloomer. But I'll be happy to be the last one that has a junior.

My ship has set sail but still sitting in the bay.

My patience has the key to turn the world day by day.

I'll be late getting there.

Denouement of Sin

Its pain I never showed.

Stories I never told.
They say beauty is in the eyes of the beholder, so behold it.

The scars are never healed.
The wounds stayed opened.

When it looked like it was over, I kept faith and kept hoping.

From going through the motions

Anger and agitation.

To live young and reckless.
To hand claps at graduation.

Opportunity waiting, and Satan kept on hating.
So he dug up all the dirt he thought could kill my reputation

Assassinate my character, annihilate my dreams.
These times they make you stronger, as hopeless as it seems.
My storm wet the pages, I turn them into 16s.
And my peace becomes still like the oceans and the seas.

This mic is all I ever need to vent to, if you only knew my
struggles, take a walk into my shoes.

Born to be a sinner, my past is just my past, this is the story of
Vash.

I'll end up first, even if I start last.
The years passes by, I calculate and do the math.

Sorting through my memories, reaching for my lifeline.
Might do it for the vine and make 6 seconds last a lifetime.

Regret and mistakes are all I've ever known, that's why these
battle scars are all I've ever sewn.

Mind over matter, wisdom is my greatest weapon.
And if I ever go to hell, I'm tall enough to reach heaven.

Battle Scars

Life was going smooth until you hit a roadblock, and that was
around the same time that the smiles stopped.

No more road, can't find your way. Your home is gone,
nowhere for your head to lay.

Where did I go wrong, what could I have done right?
Tears cover my face, but pain fuels my sight.

I use to tell you I love you, I'm so confused. You don't feel the
same, straight up out the blue.

But with my shining light, now it's turned black.
Can't function your whole life off track.

It's hard to believe life goes on, she is not texting back looking at your phone.

Clean the wound with music, the alcohol you abuse it. Every day is just another struggle, magic lost you nothing more than a muggle.

Never going to be the same, can't go back the way you came. Head up, facing what's next. Your next move just has to be your best.

Shadow

With this one, I couldn't figure out where to begin. So, I just let the pain take control of the pen.

You left before I could even say goodbye. Don't think I even would have the words for you even if I tried.

Shock and confusion hit me before the anger did. And apparently everyone saw it before I even did.

I use to admire you, and look up to you. Since your personality overshadowed mine, I couldn't see through you. I just wish I knew before it started so I could have gotten through to you.

My equal, my partner in crime till you took it too far and committed a crime. And if I was your lawyer I could not defend you.

Have a lot of friends, but few best. None of them I called my twin. Blood couldn't make us closer, but choices led this relationship to a complicated mess.

How do you move on when your very own commits the highest treason? Now my niece is all messed up, and you are the sole reason.

Was she the first...? Stop I don't even want to know. It hurts that I ever called you bro.

I get sore at the mere mention of your name. So how the hell do you think I feel writing this, and sharing this with world?

They say that a shared pain is a pain healed, so I hope this is the remedy that I need. Confessing myself to this body of work, tattooing it all until my pen bleeds.

September 17th (2017)

"What do you mean you aren't happy?" I asked

"I haven't been in years, I just can't take it anymore" she
replied with tears in her eyes.

"But…but we were just smiling and laughing last night" I said
confused, the pain in my heart was starting to feel tight.

She looked into the window before looking back at me. "I
faked it, but now I can't fake it any longer." She said.

Silence filled the room as water fills a cup.

A cup with cracks in it, eventually it was just us again.

I was trying to find the words to say, but every time I thought I
had something.
The thought of you unhappy for so long took them right away.

Her voice broke the silence like the wind on a hot day.

"You've been nothing but kind to me, showed me things I
never knew. Took me to places, challenged me to be a better
me. I appreciated all of that. It's just that I thought when we
got together it would be a summer fling, and you started to go
above and beyond...this whole thing I wasn't ready for. It was
too much, too soon. And you were so happy, I lit up your day,
and I didn't want to take that away from you. I couldn't do
that. Then, you fell in love with me." She said silently.

Tears ran down her face, she couldn't look me in the eye.

All of this time, and she didn't even feel the same.
While I was smiling in the sunshine, she was walking in the
rain.

So many thoughts rushed through my head.

"You never loved me!?" I yelled, it charged out of my soul.

"Not like that. No, I care about you. I do love you. I'm just not
in love with you." She replied.

You would have thought I it did before, but at that moment
my heart was broken.
I looked down trying to find an answer as to why this was
happening.
But every time I thought about it, it became more saddening.

49

"I'm sorry, I never meant to hurt you…I" she muttered. "All this time, and you say you didn't mean to hurt me? You've been lying to me this whole time!" I yelled at her. "You've been using me this whole time. I gave you everything. I was good to you. I was perf…"

"Perfect?! Perfect? You were a lot of things, but you were not perfect. A lot of the things you did to get me, you slowly stopped doing. On top of that, your problem was that you cared too much about being perfect. I may have lied to you, but you've been lying to yourself. It's like you got a damn robot. You eat, sleep and breathe this relationship but in the same breath, you haven't been who you really are since we got together." She snapped back.

Her words hit home like monthly bill that she came to collect.
Always tried my best, but her requirements weren't met.

She said I was a robot, and my emotions weren't my own.
I helped construct a kingdom with a sand castled throne.

Did I always know it subconsciously?
How could something so profound be unknown to me?

So here we are standing in a room with all our faults.
The mess we're in are both of our faults.
Guess we ended before we began, death to the work of the proposal plan…

Back Before Dreams

Too much heart, not enough soul.

Thoughts drowning in liquor, but it only makes the words that much more bold.

The thing that I've become is unfamiliar but, yet it feels like home.

Sitting on the outside for so long just to feel the definition of the word belong.

The things that would have kept me up at night now sleep in my bed.

And if ignorance is bliss, I keep my heart fed.

Where's my conscience when I need him.

Guess he's just hanging out with my old imaginary friends, George and Tim.

Use to have my nose in the books, and not care about my looks.

Now, I buy the sweetest candy and keep my nose clean.

When did I become this person, this person of doubt? If I did have a voice of reason, I'm sure I'd ignore the sound.

Winter

Headphones

Play, next, forward, shuffle. I'm trying to move my music
around.

I don't have time for a pause these days, I'm trying to block out
that heartbreak sound.

The world tells me I'll be alright that it's just a phase.

My mom said she didn't like her in the first place.

The guys say go and get another one and treat 'em like lays.

But no one can tell you how to cope with your own pain.

They think they understand, but you just can't wipe out memories like a stain.

This music I blast through these headphones are the only thing that are keeping me going.

Sometimes your phone is your best friend, it knows just what to play. It knows just what to say.

It can help you fight back your tears, everything is influential in your ears.

Headphones always blast the best songs because everything the world plays is trying to knock you off your throne.

And suddenly It doesn't hurt as much as it did before, and those wounds have become scars.

Bus Stop

I've been on this bus for so long, my original dream escaped me. Been happy for everyone else, only those left got hate for me.

Seeing everyone get off at their destination well before I have, hasn't been good for my psyche.

To see people, do more with less than you. I've done more but I still have a lot to prove.

I envy you for making something of yourself, facing fears, working hard, and earning for yourself.

I'm afraid to do what I have to do. What if I fail and that's the end of the line. As long as I stay in this seat, I'm fine.

But I want to be better, want to be the key to open my own secret treasure.

Too busy counting your blessings instead of minding my own. Can't take the criticism, I'm addicted to the negativity that comes from my phone.

Will I even have the same support that I've been giving people the longest? When did I allow my mental to let all these set in.

Eventually, the bus driver will announce this is the last stop. Maybe then, I'll get the courage to climb when I'm at the bottom and the only view is at the top.

The Search

There have always been people searching for something more, something that they never had before.

Where will your search take you? To the beaches off long shore, or even all the way to the earth's core?

We are all looking to be loved and accepted by somebody, but we end up looking in all the wrong places.

We think love is there and we just dump ourselves into somebody who really doesn't even care. And they put us through so much that we cannot even bear.
And then we go crying to God, complaining to him that it's not fair.

I've come to a conclusion that you can't fall for an illusion and our love ends up with an intruder that has stolen our heart.

And even if you love me and have fallen in love with me that was once, remember that it's all a learning experience.

Don't go looking for love because somehow someway it'll find you and you'll know when it finally does.

Because just like a couple of sips of gin, you'll certainly feel a buzz. You'll know that cupid has come and gone again.

The Worst in Me

Use to be all smiles and fireworks, now it's all gloom and waterworks.

Betrayals were all I was presented with.

I'm halfway through this bottle when the tears hit.

You're bad for me but your lies intoxicate.

Hearts an open sore, your soldiers invade.

They say you never know what you got till it's gone.

I'm a love-sick puppy trying to get home.

Looking at our old pictures on my phone,

It's the only way I won't ever feel alone.

I'm such a shell of the man I used to be.

Your love is a jail, can't break free from it.
Trying to recollect what's left

Cuz it's getting hard to recognize myself.

Don't need, but want you, I'm a contradiction.

It would have been so easy if this was all fiction.

The Yoda

I use to think life was so clear, then I met a dear who was at
one time a fawn.

Then things got complicated, I lost my way but eventually
found my railroad.

Along the way, people tried to sell me things that would be a
burden to my soul.

Ball for 365, then my life would only revolve around 81,
cameras flash for 24 but all the life's pleasures would amount
to "x"

My mom told me not to accept candy from a stranger so why
would I take sugarcoated shit bar from you.

We're so different, we could both wear glasses and drink from
a half empty cup and still have our different views.

I'm an asshole but I've never showed my ass because I know
better.
I wish I could just use excuses but fortunately my mind has
been built to better.

It's whispers among the town, but they look up to the great
oak.

Trying to figure out a path of their own.
The ones at the top never forget what it looks like.
But the ones that waits on a shooting star will never know what
it looks like.

This poem might go over your heads but that's why you have
hands to catch it

Use your own conclusion to match it.

Failed to Succeed

Today, I failed to succeed. I ran out of time on the clock. Held the ball when I had the last shot.

Stood there all prepared, all in disgust even though I really cared about the outcome. The time I invested wasn't worth the income.

Today, I failed to succeed. Not because I wanted to. But because I had to.

Life is all about opportunity. And I failed to take advantage.
Failed to let go.
All to be left with hope.

Today, I failed to succeed. Laziness is a drug that I over abused. Honestly, I wished my procrastination would have slowed my addiction, but my fear was on a mission to expose my greatest strengths.

Today, I failed to succeed where others have succeeded to fail.

I put the final nail in the coffin to make the transition from failing to succeeding. I had to find the win in the loss. The price was well worth the cost.

Today I failed to succeed.

Confessions of an under-construction heart.

They cry tears of pain and I turn to be the issue.

I use to take everybody's burdens and make them my own and that was an issue.

I'm skinny but carried the weight of the world, that's what it felt like.

I thought carrying it all was my call of duty.

But I can do more just lending an ear, and that's my Halo Reach.

And it's funny because back then I was an asshole.

So selfish, hurt some of the ones I love the most.

Karma came back and got me good and it made me open my eyes.

Even the best of us fall from grace.

There wasn't towel clean enough to wash the pain from my face.

I had to learn to be human, after acting like I was holier than though.

My lips would form, but it still showed through my smile.

Had a stadium full of ride or die.

But now circle comfortably sits in my 2 doors.

Wish I could say the same for me.

My friends say I should get out and do more.

But I like my "Me" time and sometimes, dealing with others is a chore.

But I can't help but think if they're right and I'm just existing.

I talk to God and ask him for direction.

My heart is torn into two, but my mind is trying to keep it all together and push through.

I think too much and that only adds to the problem.

But I need to think of ways to solve them.

Guess this is all part of growing up.

I'm 21 and still trying to find myself.

Rather go through this now than when I'm older.

Marching through the trials and tribulations like a soldier.

Far from perfect, but I embrace my imperfections.

Forever grateful for all of my blessings.

I guess me saying all of this right here and now is a start.

This is the confession of Under construction heart.

S.M.H.

Clouds above my head.

Thinking of words, I shouldn't have said.

I'm just trying to find myself. Kind of hard when you don't know where to start.

She said she'd take me to the city of Angels.

But she left me in the state of Depression.

When I lost you, I lost a part of myself.

And it's like time stood still. My life sitting on a shelf.

Spending my time deciding what's next.

I've made a lot of mistakes and I'm trying to make amends.

Going to church asking God to show me the path. Amen.

Well there's no use in sleeping in depression.

I've been through hell and back. I have learned my lessons.

Opening the door that was closed until now.

And walking through this thing called life.

I'm just SMH, Searching for My Halo

Kinda Funny

I wish I could tell you exactly who I am, but at age of 26, I'm still trying to figure that out for myself.

When I was a kid, I always imagined at this age I'd be happy and have plenty of wealth, plethora of friends, and impeccable health.

I have neither, and I've never felt as close to reality.

To have everything is to have nothing at all and having nothing means there's always something to gain.

I left everything behind for the moment, and the moment became years, which in turn brought long nights and tears.

Poisoning myself, consuming things I didn't need. Going places because of the fear of missing out. Watching fans become peers and began to wallow in self-doubt.

Kind of funny, I had to fall from grace, to appreciate fall from grace. Wrote my future in 2010, never would have thought of it.

A glimpse of hope, from learning from my mistakes. 2nd chance in front of me, damn right I went ahead and bought it.

I don't deserve your kindness, let alone your forgiveness. I can't promise you that I won't fail again at some point. But I can promise you I can only get better.

This is only the beginning, the first paragraph at the start of a love letter. For better or for worse, I'm back here again. I've lost it all before, so the only thing left is to win...

Disappointed Stan

My hero growing up was a college dropout.

Mimicked your style of polos and bookbags. Couldn't tell me nothing. In you, I found my swag.

Your creativity I admired, I was always in awe. Put you on the highest pedestal, I had no idea one day you would fall.

Spazz after spazz, most of us turned a blind eye. Giving you all the excuses, because we never wanted you to die.

After your mom passed, you've never been quite the same. How could you even heal while dealing with all the flashing lights of the fame.

We were worried and just wanted the best for you. But how could we help, when you made more messes for yourself?

What even hurts more is that your art suffered for it. Long gone was the creative and the innovative.

Now we're left with your inaccurate facts and red maga hats.

My hero lived long enough to see himself become the villain. A small piece of me hopes you'll redeem yourself lord willing.

The method to your madness is something only you can see. The rest of us are blinded by the ultralight beam.

December 29th (2018)

When I was with you, I didn't have an identity. The problem was that I hoped to find one when you were with me.

I wanted to be everything to make you happy, silly me that only made it the opposite.

I blamed you for everything for so long that with the void in me I adopted darkness.

I didn't know who I was but am sure as hell knew who I wasn't. But that didn't matter because it took the pain away.

But through that, I figured out my true character as a man. Everything I'm not, made me everything I am.

Had to fall from grace, just to figure out my place. Had to wander through the darkness to appreciate the light.

Years later, I became the person that I should have been to you back then. Sometimes, I want to pick up the phone and try to give us a second wind.

But to do that would seem like a step backwards. We're at different points now, but on the same map.

But if fate meets us together again and we're both ready, I'll gladly take your hand. Looking into the unknown, we'll proudly stand.

From yin and yang, to a saint and a sinner.
2 sides of the same coin. We'll always be Black December.

Castle Walls

My social is a façade I like to show to keep my self-esteem
high.
On the other side of the screen, there's nothing but tears.

I've screamed for help so many times in silence, that when it's
time to talk I'm hoarse.
I mean at this point it's been going on for so long, I should let
nature take its course.

Nobody checks on the strong friend because he's too busy
uplifting.
Walking through the mud of my castle tracking it everywhere
trying not to trip.

How can someone surrounded by love really be in so much
pain.
Maybe I reject it, and dance alone in the cold rain.

Part of me wants help, the other half is telling me to man up.
What's left drowns it out with tequila.

Slowly killing myself to help everyone around me.
Self-loath is my trusted partner, I'm in love with the idea of
being a martyr.

Too nice and understanding, I thought that would make me a
better man.
Once I took a drink from that well, its myself that I have
damned.

The weights that I lift these days are pulling my lips back to
smile.
Just because it's strong doesn't mean it's healthy.

"well why don't you just let us in, ask for help?"
It takes strength that I no longer possess.

Everyone thinks it's easy to just pull yourself up
But nobody knows how heavy you are.

I wish I had your optimism. Your hope.

Still I will keep on this crusade, and provide you shade from
the sun.

I will bare these scars, until It's time to return to my kingdom come.

Home

This feeling is something I haven't felt in years.

The excitement, the passion, the love.

Back then, I use to put the pen to the paper.

Now, my fingers dance all across the screen

I can tell that you missed my touch, my voice

The way I bare all of my emotions, my scars, and my truths.

You were always there, how could I leave something that always held me down?

I clipped our wings when we were almost at our peak.

Suddenly, wings weren't as interesting, and I just wanted to use my feet.

How can I tell you sorry if I kinda don't regret it?

I had to see what I could do all on my own.

Had to grow apart, so I could grow up, and eventually get back to you so I can show you how much I've grown.

But just abandoning you wasn't right either. I'll apologize for that.

I'm hoping you can forgive me, for the things that I've done.

I'm back now, I'm home now, and I promise I'll never leave you again.

You might have needed me to express these thoughts, but I needed you to see these thoughts without judgment or malice.

Now mind you, these are 'Spoken,' not words because I need my journey to be read. Hopefully, now at the end of it all you truly know Fred...

Made in the USA
Monee, IL
03 April 2020

24383191R00044